Rainforest

Written by Steve Parker
Edited by Natalie Munday and Sarah Powell
Designed by Chris Fraser and Nicola Friggens

priddy books
big ideas for little people

Warm and wet

Tropical rainforests are some of the warmest, wettest places on Earth. Their mix of moisture and heat mean many different kinds of plants grow closely together. There are tiny flowers as small as rice grains, and giant trees as tall as skyscrapers, with trunks wider than enormous trucks. Everywhere there is a tangle of leaves, roots, shoots, and stems.

Flowers

Trees

Animals

Lots of plants mean lots of animals, too. There are **millions** of bugs, snails, ants, and worms smaller than this "o." **Enormous** elephants stroll silently among the trees, and peaceful gorillas chew leaves and fruit. But **dangers** lurk here, as fierce big cats prowl the forest floor and eagles swoop overhead. Nowhere else on Earth has **wildlife** that is so fascinating, so beautiful, and so deadly.

Endangered rating:

The leaf ratings show how endangered rainforest life is due to logging, pollution, humans, and other threats.

1	2	3	4	5
least endangered				most endangered

To show how big the animals and plants are, you can compare their sizes to an adult.

If they are small, we use an adult hand instead.

Rainforests from around the world

The Amazon

The biggest rainforest in the world, the Amazon, covers the same total area as all the other rainforests put together! It can also rain here for more than 200 days a year.

Madagascar

Madagascar has some of the world's strangest and rarest rainforest animals. They include many types of lemurs, flying fox bats, and even tomato frogs!

The Congo

The Congo is the second biggest rainforest, with over 1,000 kinds of birds, 300 types of reptiles, and 12,000 species of plants. The endangered mountain gorilla also lives here.

Rainforests are found all over the Earth, from the tropical rainforests of Central America to the cool forests of New Zealand's South Island. Tropical rainforests are near to the Equator in an area called the tropics. It's warm or hot every day, sometimes over 104°F (40°C)! Temperate, or cool, rainforests, are far away from the tropics, farther north and south. The temperature here is cooler and can fall as low as 41°F (5°C).

Pacific Coast

These temperate rainforests are found along the northwest coast of North America. They have warm—not hot—summers, and cool—not cold—winters.

Tasmania

South of mainland Australia, the island of Tasmania has temperate forests. Creatures such as the fierce Tasmanian devil hunt in the cool darkness.

Borneo

Over half this beautiful island in Southeast Asia is covered in rainforest. At over 120 million years old, these are older than almost any other forests in the world.

These **gentle** apes spend most of their lives in the branches of trees, sitting quietly as they munch **plant foods.** Their favorites are fruit, especially **durians,** which smell horrible to humans! Orangutans tend to live alone, except for **mothers,** who care for their young for up to seven years.

Large brain in relation to body size

Flexible shoulders and arms for climbing

Fact file

Size, up to: 5 ft (1.5 m) tall

Lives: Borneo and Sumatra, Southeast Asia

Endangered rating:
🌿 🌿 🌿 🌿 🌿

Fun fact
"Orangutan" is a Malaysian word that means "person of the forest."

Orangutan

The red-eyed tree frog is **nocturnal.** It sleeps by day, then hunts by night for moths, flies, and similar bugs. If a predator, such as a snake, comes near, the resting tree frog opens wide its big, red **eyes.** This confuses **predators,** giving the tree frog enough time to **leap** to safety.

Fun fact
The frog's toe pads are so sticky, it can walk up windows.

Green body blends in with leaves

Tree frog

Fact file

Size: Mostly less than 2 in (5 cm) long

Lives: Central and South America

Endangered rating:

Toucan

Beak can be a third of its body length

Fun fact

A noisy flock of squawking toucans can be heard over 1 mile (1.6 km) away!

Bright yellow neck and chest

With its big, bright beak, the **keel-billed** toucan looks so front heavy, it seems like it would topple over! However, its beak actually has lots of tiny **air holes** inside like a sponge, meaning it weighs very little. These toucans live in **small groups** and eat a varied diet, including berries, insects, and even a **lizard** or two!

Giant flower

The world's biggest flower grows in Southeast Asia's rainforests. The Rafflesia (Raff-leez-ee-ah), or corpse flower, looks and smells like rotten flesh. Its foul smell attracts flies and insects that then help the flower to reproduce by carrying its pollen to other Rafflesia flowers.

Smell comes from central chamber

Fact file

Size, up to:
3 ft (90 cm) across

Lives:
Southeast Asia

Endangered rating:

Folded-back outer petals

Brown pattern mimics rotting flesh

Wandering Spider

Never go near a Brazilian wandering spider, as it has one of the most **deadly** bites of any creature in the world! This big, strong spider does not spin a **web.** Instead it wanders along the forest floor at night, its **fangs** ready to **bite** and kill any unsuspecting rat or beetle!

Scarlet red hairs cover its fangs

Fact file

Size, up to:
6 in (15 cm) across legs

Lives:
Central and South America

Endangered rating:

Jaguars are the **largest** big cats in Central and South America. They are strong **predators** and kill all kinds of animals, from small mice to large deer. Unlike most other big cats, they are good **swimmers** and hunt prey such as turtles, water snakes, and caimans (a type of crocodile) in the **rivers** of the rainforest.

Pattern blends with forest shade

Fun fact
The jaguar is such a powerful predator, it can kill prey with one bite!

Fact file
Size, up to:
8 ft (2.4m) nose to tail

Lives:
Central and South America

Endangered rating:
🌿 🌿 🌿 🌿 🌿

Jaguar

Although it may look like a large **pig,** the Malayan tapir is actually more closely related to rhinos and **horses.** While its black-and-white **coloring** is easy to see in the open, at night in the shadowy undergrowth of the rainforest, this bulky animal becomes almost **invisible.**

Black-and-white
fur pattern

Long
bendable
snout

Tapir

Fact file

Size, up to:
8 ft (2.4 m) head to body

Lives: Mainland Southeast Asia and Sumatra

Endangered rating:
🌿 🌿 🌿 🌿 🌿

Tap, tap, tap...the sound of an aye-aye looking for grubs and bugs at `night` among the rainforest branches. It taps the wood and listens for a `hollow` sound, which shows that a juicy grub is living in a hole inside. The aye-aye tears off the bark, `pokes` its very long middle finger into the `hole,` and pulls out the tasty meal.

Fun fact

Aye-ayes are very rare and can only be found on the island of Madagascar.

Yellow eyes see in the dark

Very long middle finger

Aye-aye

Birdwing

Long antennae (feelers)

Spotted pattern on underwings

The world's **biggest** butterfly, the Queen Alexandra's birdwing, is found in Papua New Guinea. It flutters in the **sunshine** amongst the rainforest's topmost twigs and **branches,** and then settles on newly open flowers to sip their sugary **nectar** and rest in the leaves.

Fact file

Size, across wings:
Females: 12 in (30 cm)

Lives: Southeast Asia (Papua New Guinea)

Endangered rating:
🌿 🌿 🌿 🌿 🌿

Rhino

One of the world's `rarest` animals, the Sumatran rhinoceros only lives in a few `places` in Southeast Asia. It hides away in the thickest, most `remote` rainforest and likes to lean on young trees, `pushing` them over to reach their soft, lush leaves.

This young rhino's horn will grow bigger

Very strong sense of smell

Fact file

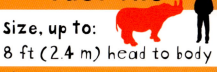

Size, up to:
8 ft (2.4 m) head to body

Lives: About six small areas in Southeast Asia

Endangered rating:
🌿 🌿 🌿 🌿 🌿

Fun fact

Sumatran rhinos are the smallest of the five kinds of rhinoceros.

Harpy eagle

One of the biggest eagles, the harpy, flies just above the rainforest treetops—so, monkeys and sloths, watch out! At any moment this huge winged hunter may swoop down, grab its prey in its fiercely sharp talons (claws), and carry it back to its nest.

Feathers spread for slow flight

Talons folded back

Fact file

Size, up to:
7 ft (2.1 m) across wings

Lives:
Central and South America

Endangered rating:

Fun fact

A harpy eagle can fly away with prey as heavy as itself—over 17 lb (8 kg).

This panther chameleon is hard to notice because its **colors** blend so well with leaves and bark. If a fly or moth lands nearby, then flick! This lizard's amazing **tongue,** as long as its body, **shoots** out to grab the prey. The tongue's **sticky** tip then pulls the food back into the lizard's mouth.

Body covered with small scales

Fun fact
The chameleon's eyes move separately. It can look in front and behind at the same time!

Split feet grip either side of branch

Chameleon

Okapi

Large ears for good hearing

Legs have zebra like stripes

Fun fact
The okapi's tongue is so long, it can clean its own ears, outside and inside!

While their stripes look a lot like a zebra's, okapi are actually more closely related to giraffes. This shy animal is rarely seen in the wild and usually lives alone. Okapi spend their days chewing all kinds of leaves, fruits, and bark, as well as poisonous toadstools, but will hide amongst bushes at night.

Army ants **swarm** in lines along the forest floor, **attacking** almost any food from small bugs, snails, and worms to larger creatures like frogs, lizards, small birds, and even mammals! **Hundreds** of them sting, bite, kill, and cut up each victim together. They then share their **food** with the whole group.

Tough body casing

Long jaws cut up prey

Fun fact
At night army ants cluster together as a "living nest" to protect their queen.

Army ants

The fruits of the cacao tree are brown pods that contain **seeds** called cacao **beans.** They are very important as we use them to make **chocolate!** These trees are still found in the wild, but most are now grown on farms or plantations all around the **tropics.**

Fun fact

It takes about ten cacao beans to make one small bar of chocolate!

Fact file

Size, up to:
25 ft (7.6 m) tall

Lives: Originally Central and South America, now all tropics

Endangered rating:
🌿 🌿 🌿 🌿 🌿

There are around 20–40 beans in each pod

Cacao tree

Spider monkey

Fact file

Size, up to: 2.5 ft (75 cm) head to body

Lives: Eastern South America

Endangered rating:
🌿 🌿 🌿 🌿 🌿

The woolly spider monkey can eat with both its hands and feet at the same time, by hanging from a branch by its tail. The tail is prehensile, meaning it can curl around things and grip them strongly. Also known as the muriqui, this monkey can travel from tree to tree, leaping more than 70 ft (21 m) between branches.

Toes grasp like fingers

Fun fact

This monkey's tail grows up to 30 in (80 cm)—that's longer than its head and body together.

Vampire bat

Large ears

Thin, sharp teeth

Fun fact
If a vampire bat cannot feed itself, others at its roost "sick up" some blood for it!

As the moon rises, vampire bats leave their roost (resting place) in a cave or tree hole. They seek out warm-blooded animals such as deer, horses, and cows for a tasty meal. The bat lands, crawls next its victim, then slices off a small piece of skin with its razor-sharp front teeth. It then laps up the warm, red, oozing blood.... Mmm, mmm.

"To-kay!" calls the tokay gecko when it wants to find a mate for breeding. These lizards have multicolored spots of cream, yellow, orange, and red on a green or blue background. They can make their spots lighter or darker, among tree leaves or old twigs on the forest floor, in order to hide from predators.

Wide mouth swallows bugs and similar prey

Strong clawed toes grip bark

Fact file
Size, up to: 16 in (40 cm) nose to tail

Lives: Southern and Southeast Asia

Endangered rating:

Tokay gecko

Burmese python

Few creatures can escape the death <mark>coils</mark> of the Burmese python. It wraps its <mark>long</mark> body around its prey, slowly <mark>squeezing</mark> its coils tighter and tighter. Once the prey is dead, the snake begins to swallow it <mark>whole,</mark> even if it's as big as a wild pig or goat!

Strong body muscles

Patterned skin matches forest floor leaves

Fun fact

A python that eats a big meal may not be hungry again for three months!

Fact file

Size, up to:
18 ft (5.5 m) long

Lives:
Southern and Southeast Asia

Endangered rating:

Like a fat worm, the leech **wriggles** and loops to find a warm-blooded victim to stick onto with its two **suckers**, one at each end of its body. Its mouth, in the front sucker, has tiny **teeth** to slice the victim's skin, then the leech can suck its fill of blood, **swelling** up like a red balloon.

Mouth is in its sucker

Thick muscular body

Fact file

Size, up to:
18 in (45 cm) long

Lives:
All tropical rainforests

Endangered rating:

Leech

Rainforests at risk

Nowhere else has more amazing wildlife, with different kinds of creatures and plants, than tropical rainforests. But all around the world, they are in danger of being destroyed. This is known as deforestation.

Logging is one of the biggest threats to rainforests. People cut down trees to sell the timber (wood).

Rare creatures are at great **risk.** They might be caught alive and sold as **exotic** pets, but many die. These animals may also be killed and eaten by people, which is known as the **bushmeat trade.**

As the human **population** grows, more people need places to live, and more food to eat. Rainforests are **cleared** for **villages,** towns, and land for crops and farm animals.

Glossary

Antennae Feelers on the head of animals such as insects, centipedes, and crabs.

Cold-blooded A creature that cannot make heat inside its body to keep itself warm, so it is usually the same temperature as its surroundings.

Deforestation Cutting down trees in forests, usually for their wood or timber, and to clear land for farming or other human uses.

Endangered A creature at risk of dying out, or being killed off.

Equator An imaginary line around the middle of the Earth at its widest point, midway between the North Pole and South Pole.

Nectar Sweet sugary liquid made by flowers to attract bugs and other creatures who spread the flowers pollen.